AF583624

WRITERS

ON

WRITERS

Published in partnership with

WRITERS GEORDIE WILLIAMSON ON ALEXIS WRIGHT WRITERS

Published by Black Inc.
in association with the University of Melbourne and State Library Victoria

Black Inc., an imprint of Schwartz Books Pty Ltd
Wurundjeri Country
22–24 Northumberland Street, Collingwood VIC 3066, Australia
enquiries@blackincbooks.com
www.blackincbooks.com

State Library Victoria
328 Swanston Street, Melbourne VIC 3000, Australia
www.slv.vic.gov.au

The University of Melbourne
Parkville VIC 3010, Australia
www.unimelb.edu.au

9781760645632 (hardback)
9781743824191 (ebook)

A catalogue record for this work is available from the National Library of Australia

Cover design by Peter Long and Aira Pimping
Typesetting by Marilyn de Castro
Photograph of Alexis Wright by Vincent Leonard Long

The epigraphs on p. vi are excerpts from Wendell Berry, 'How to Be a Poet', *Given: Poems*, New York: Counterpoint Press, 2006, and Oodgeroo Noonuccal, 'No More Boomerang', *The Dawn Is at Hand: Poems*, Brisbane: Jacaranda Press, 1966.

Printed in China by 1010 Printing.

For Ivor, *Il miglior editore*

There are no unsacred places;
there are only sacred places
and desecrated places

Wendell Berry

Black hunted wallaby,
White hunt dollar;
White fella witch-doctor
Wear dog-collar.

Oodgeroo Noonuccal

No Australian novel opens like *Carpentaria*. Scratch that, I'll go further. No narrative of any kind, from any time or place, opens like *Carpentaria* – besides, perhaps, the Book of Genesis:

> The ancestral serpent, a creature larger than storm clouds, came down from the stars, laden with its own creative enormity. It moved graciously – if you had been watching with the eyes of a bird hovering in the sky far above the ground. Looking down at the serpent's wet body, glistening from the ancient sunlight, long before man was a creature who could contemplate the next moment in time. It came down those billions of years ago, to crawl on its heavy belly, all around the wet clay soils in the Gulf of Carpentaria.

Wright describes the Rainbow Serpent as it sets about scouring the tidal mudflats, boring riverine capillaries deep into the landscape. So vast are its undulations that an entire delta is inscribed upon the region before the serpent finally ceases its labours, coming to rest beneath a waterway, a river hallowed by its subterranean guest:

> This is where the giant serpent continues to live deep down under the ground in a vast network of limestone aquifers. They say its being is porous; it permeates everything. It is all around in the atmosphere and is attached to the lives of the river people like skin.

This is the creation story that Alexis Wright, a woman of the Waanyi nation, arrays against that of an imported, imposed Christianity. *In the beginning was the Word* reflects an important difference: 'logos' first, world second. For fallen creatures, a connection to nature is necessarily second-hand.

For Waanyi, that same world is intimate, interpenetrating.

Carpentaria is a fiction that opens in the auditory landscape of church bells that have, since the arrival of missionaries to the region, regimented the lives of the Gulf's original inhabitants, marking white time and white ways. They are a group who suffer the strictures of religion without receiving the grace of Christ, a painful and enraging fact. Among them, writes Wright, are little girls 'who come home from Church on Sunday, who look around themselves at the human fallout and announce matter-of-factly, *Armageddon begins here*'.

~

How should we understand the story that opens *Carpentaria* – the story that in one way or another all of Wright's fiction tells? We might say that hers are a series of counter-myths. They assert the primacy and appropriateness of Indigenous story and lore in an antipodean context (as well as a planetary one). Her body of work constitutes an epic *revelation* of First Peoples' fusion with place – and a reckoning of the costs that come from severing that connection.

We could also say that these counter-myths are the necessary precondition for counter-*power*: Wright's imagination works to bolster and justify real-world moral, political and legal claims made by Indigenous Australians against racism and government fiat. Her novels describe an ongoing struggle for justice. They dramatise the tensions that flow when duelling political frameworks coexist in a single geographic domain.

So it is that Wright wields a Western literary form to depict the ongoing erasure of First Nations culture and the resulting anger and despair of its people, and to notate and decry ecological devastation brought about by the colonial project over time, whether local and particular (feral donkeys) or global and abstract (climate change).

Beyond this, Wright deploys a particular set of approaches to the novel – the kind of sprawling, fabulist, experimental forms we associate with Latin American magical realism and European modernism – not only for formal effect but as an expression of the alternative ontological grounds of Indigenous existence. Alexis Wright doesn't just want to alter Australia's political valency. She aims to overthrow our way of being in the world.

~

These are large claims to make on behalf of an otherwise modest and even retiring person. I've had the good fortune to know Alexis Wright for some years now. I can attest to her gentleness and wry humour, her deep sense of obligation and her dislike of fuss. But as a close reader of Wright's novels – a superfan, really – I also register her anger on the page. It's fury that can glow incandescent when considering the abject situation of her fellows, or any who are downtrodden and dispossessed.

In such moments she reminds me of Maria Callas's startling, kohl-eyed portrayal of the title character in *Medea*, Pier Pasolini's 1969 film adaptation of Euripides' play – a work in which the sorceress's outward wrath is expressed through, even supercharged by, an inward command and grace. Both Medea/Callas and Alexis have earned, with every fibre, their outrage.

But it's not only a matter of being composed in affront. Alexis is also widely and deeply read, with literary tastes that are unexpected, subtle and catholic. In T.S. Eliot's admiring formulation, she doesn't borrow from the best of past and contemporary writing; she *steals*. More than this, she is diligent in her own practice. I've no idea how she's found time, over the years, to produce work of such quality and scale.

This combination of passion and perseverance, grit and experiment, has taken Wright from outback community activist to local favourite for the Nobel Prize. It has made her one of the best-known and justly celebrated Australian novelists of the twenty-first century. It has also made her a stand-in for broader controversies – a lightning rod for arguments both political and aesthetic. I sometimes suspect she's an author more worried over than read and, when read, more often misconstrued than *got*.

This book is intended as a defence of Alexis Wright's art – a body of work I regard as being without precedent in contemporary world literature – and a celebration of its virtues. It's also an account of the radical implications her art holds for how we live together, even understand the world. To do so, I'm obliged to assume some unorthodox critical stances, moving from close reading of Wright's novels to broader editorialising – tacking between classical Roman curse poems and John Howard's 'Intervention', European fairy tales and the animist turn of contemporary jurisprudence. I've had to unlearn a great deal and start from scratch in these pages – all in the hope that you, dear reader, will join me in exploring the exhilarating range of possibilities Wright's work presents.

~

On Alexis Wright starts out from twinned premises. The first concerns philistinism. Australian readers, raised on a diet of anti-intellectualism and Anglo empiricism, tend to read in instrumental ways. We want our literature to tell us stuff, efficiently and neatly. I think of the man who bailed up Alexis at an event for her fourth novel, *Praiseworthy*, seeking clarification. He'd read the 700-plus-page book from beginning to end in a matter of days, he said, and didn't understand it. As Australian literature scholar Bernadette Brennan drolly responded on hearing this story, 'If that's how you're reading Alexis, you're *not doing it right*.'

Brennan was making a serious point. When the American Beat poet and essayist Gary Snyder visited Australia in the early 1980s, a Pintupi Elder took him out on Country, west of Alice Springs, in a four-wheel drive. As they drove, the man pointed out significant sites and told stories connected to them. He spoke very fast – too fast, indeed, for Snyder to capture much sense. Only after a time did Snyder realise these tales were designed to unfold at walking speed. An internal combustion engine had set the songlines on fast forward. It's like this with Alexis. Her novels can be digressive, sometimes dauntingly so – endlessly attenuating yarns with no discernible endpoint. They employ temporal schemes in which past, present and future are experienced simultaneously. Wildly varying registers of language and tone, from broad vernacular to cathedral pomp, can cohabit in the same passage. Her narratives are great menageries of stray detail in which social realism and supernaturalism sit side by side.

The traditional realist novel has not prepared us for characters like hers, the choral quality of even their private thought. Her magnificent 'collective' biography of Bruce Tilmouth, *Tracker*, unfolds like a long night by an open fire with a Chaucerian cast telling tall tales about an old, beloved friend – in triplicate. To read Alexis in the right way requires the use of a different set of mental muscles. She demands that we slow to walking speed. That's how purely, unrepentantly *analogue* she is.

Once the reader surrenders to this approach, however, Wright's novels make their own kind of sense. She is, like Patrick White before her, a prophet. She maintains obedience to a moral law that stands beyond the front office kind, and her narrators rail against the insanity of all violence fomented by humans against nature. Wright's stories traffic in paradox, as the prophets did, and they proceed by the illogic of dreams. If Western rationality has led us to the point of collective disaster, her novels suggest, then elegantly adumbrated fabulist maximalism is the only sane register to deploy. Every society, even the most pragmatic and empirically minded, such as ours, needs artists like Wright.

Philistinism is not only a discomfort with words that sit strangely on the page; it can possess a metaphysical aspect. Those of us who are neo-Europeans – plonked down on this island continent with a vexed relation to place, tragically entwined with Australia's original inhabitants – fail to appreciate histories deeper than our own. We tore ourselves free of connection to place to voyage out generations ago. It abetted our various coups during the settler-colonial era; it's also our epigenetic wound.

We find it hard, for example, to grasp that a people's historical imagination could be intuited via, even embedded in, *spatial* terms. When Indigenous Australians speak of *Country*, they refer to the accrued knowledge, stored in myth, ritual, art, law and song, of all ecological relations in a bioregion over time. It is an extraordinary matrix of meaning and connection, much of which is opaque to those of us who came after.

Just as Alexis serves as a scribe to the locals of Waanyi Country when she spends a portion of each year there, so too does her fiction serve as scribe to Country itself. Of the 1963 Yirrkala Bark Petitions – the foundational documents of the land rights movement – the Yolngu people of Arnhem Land who authored them said that they gave 'the land a tongue'. Wright should be seen in this light: as a 'medium' of *Country* across time; as one through whom ancestors speak – and not as a singular, exalted author in the modern sense.

~

My second premise will seem counterintuitive, given the deep history I outline in my first. This book is also about the beginning of a new kind of literature, not the extinction of an older one.

Some years ago, Nicolas Rothwell, journalist, author and the kind of eldritch visionary our culture occasionally throws up, gave a speech at the National Library of Australia, 'The Landscape Behind the Landscape'. In it, he laid out a remarkable thesis.

Rothwell spoke of the tradition of the farmer-poet – old as Hesiod – and wrenched it into the present, where it is alive in Australia in the work of figures such as Eric Rolls and Les Murray.

Rothwell's claim? While art and literature in the northern hemisphere were exhausted, in Australia, conceived of in its more radical potentialities at least, they were just setting out.

Rothwell spoke of a 'mystery of energy or presence' that manifests itself to some who enter the Australian landscape. Articulating a response to this 'mystery' is difficult, he argued, even impossible, using literary forms drawn from an inherited British tradition. The nineteenth-century English novel, for example, seems unsatisfactory, even inexplicable or absurd, when translated into antipodean space.

A new kind of literature in Australia, Rothwell argued, was coming into view. It was writing that sloughed off imported models and instead responded in unique ways to local conditions. Agrarian types are naturalists with skin in the game. Farming obliges them to interact intimately and for a prolonged time with their surrounding environment; their own wellbeing is tied to the health of the land. The figure of the farmer-poet may be a very old one. But shifted to a different continent, it promised to be radically new.

Rothwell's own books – ambiguous in terms of genre, discursive and mystically minded, exquisitely attuned to landscape and place – mark one possible version of this new literature. Alexis's work, I believe, marks another. She stands at the head of a tradition that may still be embryonic but is unarguably dynamic and rich with possibility; it is one, moreover, that draws from the deepest of wells.

We now know, thanks to writers and environmental historians such as Rolls, Bruce Pascoe, Charles Massey and Bill Gammage, that Australia's Indigenous peoples farmed with firesticks, cultivated crops and practised aquaculture, making them original custodians of what Gammage called 'the biggest estate on Earth'.

What the first Europeans to come to Australia saw as untouched wilderness was no such thing. It was a continent-wide managed system, shaped over immense time periods and reinforced by obligations to totem, story and lore. The song and the land were once as one – and Wright's art seeks to join them once again, using new forms to do so.

If we wish to understand the future that Alexis Wright represents, we must first look backwards – to those forces that for so long held efforts such as hers at bay.

BARRON FIELD

Literature in Australia has two beginnings. The first is immemorial, old as the first songs sung by the first peoples to have arrived more than two thousand human generations ago on the continent known as Sahul.

The second is eight generations and scarcely two centuries old: the transplantation of European literature to Australia. Yet it is the literature to emerge from this second beginning that has claimed, until very recently, precedence and prestige.

The ur-text of this Australian canon appeared in 1819, when *First Fruits of Australian Poetry* – a slender volume consisting of two poems, 'Botany-Bay Flowers' and 'The Kangaroo' – was published in Sydney. Its author was Barron Field, a Supreme Court judge of New South Wales. Though a lawyer by training, Field was a literary man at heart.

Here is the opening stanza of his 'The Kangaroo':

Kangaroo, Kangaroo!
Thou Spirit of Australia,
That redeems from utter failure,
From perfect desolation,
And warrants the creation
Of this fifth part of the Earth,
Which would seem an after-birth,
Not conceiv'd in the Beginning
(For GOD bless'd his work at first,
And saw that it was good),
But emerg'd at the first sinning,
When the ground was therefore curst:—
And hence this barren wood!

Back in England, Samuel Taylor Coleridge and William Wordsworth relished the poem – or at least they did according to Field's London friend the poet and essayist Charles Lamb, always keen for Field's updates from what the essayist called 'inauspicious unliterary Thiefland'. Few since have shared that opinion. It has been mainly held up as proof that literature in Australia began in a defensive crouch and stayed that way long afterwards.

Yet we shouldn't discount Field. He was a significant figure in the young colony. His legal decisions helped shape the nation Australia would become. Most noteworthy, according to recent scholarship, was his part in establishing a local application of the principle of *terra nullius*.

While the relevant case was concerned with dull issues of taxation, it's worth exploring in the light of Field's aesthetic responses to his time in the Colony of New South Wales. A comically dismissive poet when it came to the colony he may have been, but he had literary cred. A former theatre critic for *The Times* and a schoolfriend of editor and critic Leigh Hunt, he was a peripheral member of the British Romantic circle that centred around figures such as Lamb and Coleridge. He wrote a memoir of Wordsworth and was confident enough to suggest improvements to the poet's work. Wordsworth was sufficiently appreciative to accept them.

So, it counted that Field spent his years in New South Wales insisting on the unfeasibility of 'real' literature happening there. Poetry was impossible, he said, in a landscape without deciduous trees. As for its first peoples, Field was unable or unwilling to escape the racial thinking of his moment. The Australian Aborigine, he determined, could not be civilised.

Here, then, is the founding paradox of the second strand of Australian literature. It began in a blanket refusal of the very environment surrounding the colonists. And it denied the full humanity of that environment's original inhabitants, rendering them mute, incapable of making art or song worthy of European attention.

Most importantly, that aesthetic rejection was tied to a legal and political compact – *terra nullius* – that served to reinforce it over time through the full panoply of powers available to the colonial apparatus and, later, the nation state. A continent which had been (in Les Murray's memorable phrase) 'ruled by poetry' for tens of thousands of years would be governed by prose after 1788.

The culture that did emerge in the wake of Field was stunted. The presses of colonial Australia mainly produced a tidy, clubbable, public-facing poetry: satires for and against various grandees and officials; odes to mark births and deaths; squibs for newspaper columns; or maudlin laments with insistent rhymes. It was a literature embarrassed by the circumstances in which it found itself, derivative and dull.

There were, however, occasional glints. Eliza Hamilton Dunlop was the Irish wife of the 'Protector of Aborigines' at Penrith and Wisemans Ferry. Her poem of witness, 'The Aboriginal Mother', emerged from news of the Myall Creek massacre of Indigenous men, women and children in 1838. It sought to enter the experience of those who suffered at the hands of their murderers (a position for which she was mercilessly attacked by the newly established Fairfax press).

Or consider Daniel Deniehy, Australia's first critic of note. The son of risen convicts, he possessed a love of literature and a facility for rhetoric that served him brilliantly as a parliamentarian, where, by sheer persuasive force, he helped defeat William Charles Wentworth's efforts to create in the colonies a 'bunyip' aristocracy. Deniehy's passionate republicanism spoke to the possibility of a nation different in kind, not just style, to its British progenitor. Deniehy later died, drunk and defeated, in a Bathurst street.

And then there was Charles Harpur, who from his lonely rural situation sought to raise a national literature from scratch – reimagining the British Romantics and American Transcendentalists as models with which to do so. Judith Wright considered him the most 'many sided' Australian poet of the nineteenth century. But he, too, died disenchanted with his literary and political hopes.

Everywhere was either indifference, or else resistance, to the efforts of those who sought to think of the colonies as anything more than a brutal and relentless project of land enclosure and resource exploitation – the frenzy of which only increased with the discovery of gold after 1851.

In short, it was a society inimical to original literary and artistic creation because it had, as a first order of business, set its face against the surrounding world. Looking too closely at antipodean space would oblige its new inhabitants to consider uncomfortable truths: that the land had its own kind of beauty, for instance – or that others, preceding them, had found it beautiful and given due reverence in return.

For decades after European arrival, Sydney Harbour's Lavender Bay housed a prison hulk – a floating prison off a terrestrial one. I'm haunted by the symbol it represents: a colonial society that never attempted true landfall. And without landfall, of course, there can be no 'First Contact' – no mutual exchange that necessarily follows when strangers meet.

This, then, was a colony possessed of a flat-pack Enlightenment ideology – hell-bent on the idea of *Improvement* outlined by the intellectual worthies of eighteenth-century Britain – and a calculated narrowness of vision. I won't say its subsequent achievements weren't considerable. The effort demanded by the colonial project was immense. To have survived and even thrived in the teeth of geographic isolation and an alien environment is no small thing.

Still, as the poet Matthew Arnold put it during this same era, culture is the spiritual standard by which we understand wealth to be mere 'machinery'. If the wealth bought at such cost of toil – and pain to others, and damage to place – was spent on art, music and literature in colonial Australia, it was the imported kind, sailed in from the Old World.

No. There was something missing from the culture that sprang from the circumstances of Australia's founding. It was a lack that some of the best Australian writers of the twentieth century sensed. Poet Roland Robinson, for instance – leading representative of the Jindyworobak movement of the 1930s and '40s – believed that any true national literature in Australia would require engagement with Indigenous culture.

This insight was weakened, however, by the shallowness of its application. The Jindyworobaks were an exclusively white literary movement who presumed First Nations people to be a dying race. They appropriated language and lore in the manner of graverobbers, not sincere cultural interlocutors.

Novelist Xavier Herbert had a subtler grasp of Indigenous culture, thanks to time spent with anthropologists in the Top End and a long working proximity to peoples in that region. His 1975 novel *Poor Fellow My Country* laid down positions on issues such as land rights and reparations well in advance of their historical moment. His work also made use of emerging understanding of Indigenous kinship systems. But Herbert bent and falsified such material in the service of his own narrative ends.

Judith Wright was different, both in degree and kind. A descendent of those vigorous men who originally 'opened' the New England region of New South Wales, Wright's poetry and advocacy did much to clear space for Indigenous voices. Her decades-long friendship with and championing of poet and activist Kath Walker – the Noonuccal woman who later took the name Oodgeroo – was foundational in this regard.

It shouldn't come as a surprise that a step change in mutual respect and care should come from female artists. Wright and Oodgeroo were sisters whose shared love of Australian country was allied to hatred of those whose extractive zeal would destroy that country in the name of profit.

But even between these two, equals as artists and activists, there was tension. Oodgeroo did not enjoy those same privileges which Wright possessed by birth. Their relationship might be seen as one more halting attempt at crossing a profound cultural divide – one inscribed into laws that unbalanced even sincere efforts to do so.

How, then, in recent decades, has there been such an explosion of writing by Indigenous Australians that it has become impossible to ignore the aesthetic skill they bring to bear or the political urgency of the message their works carry? Kim Scott with the Miles Franklin–winning *Benang* in 1999 – or *That Deadman Dance* in 2010. Tony Birch's fiction, Melissa Lucashenko's kitchen-sink realism, Tara June Winch's *The Yield*. And wilder still, Alexis and her epics of Country.

Like these others, Wright presents an alternative vision of Australian place. But no one's sentences fret themselves to the contours of landscape quite like hers do, that prose swinging like a weathervane to the breeze. Her Country teems with flora and fauna, both feral and endemic. Her big-sky aesthetic, we might call it: fiction shaped by an ecological imagination without precedent in the imported literature of this continent, a plenitude that overflows the neat container of the English novel, rushing the form in new and unexpected directions.

How could such a transformation come to pass? How could this new way of looking at and writing Country suddenly appear? The Mabo decision of 1992 had, for the first time since Barron Field's application of *terra nullius*, recognised native title in Australia. It took the legal and political barriers to fall for the long-impeded poetry of Country to return. We should see Wright's fiction as a rejoinder to Field's primal snub.

Here's another ur-image from Australian literature: the opening paragraphs of Patrick White's *The Tree of Man*. They describe a man in a cart who stops in the heart of a stand of stringybark gums, somewhere amid the old Australian emptiness, halted by their size: 'These were the dominant trees in that part of the bush, rising above the involved scrub with the simplicity of true grandeur.'

White, along with Proust and Nabokov, one of the incorrigible synaesthesiasts of twentieth-century literature, uses every sense to freeze the moment into consequence:

> The man in the cart got down. He rubbed his hands together because already it was cold, a kernel of cold cloud in a pale sky, and copper in the west. On the air you could smell the frost, as the man rubbed his hands, the friction of cold skin intensified the

> coldness of the air and the solitude of that place. Birds looked from twigs, and the eyes of animals were drawn to what was happening. The man lifted a bundle from the cart.

The man takes an axe to a stringybark, scarring its trunk with a few hard swings, 'more to hear the sound than any other reason'.

> The man struck at the tree, and struck, till several white chips had fallen. He looked at the scar in the side of the tree. The silence was immense. It was the first time anything like this had happened in that part of the Bush.

It's a powerful set piece. Those axe blows cruelly announcing a fresh annexation of place. But what grants the passage force is the split between narrative perspective and actions described. While the narration works to establish the untrammelled ecological richness of this site, the unnamed character only sees timber to be used. His is the first of a series of desecrations that will see this stand of gums overwritten by the suburban sprawl of an Australian city.

These, by way of contrast, are the opening lines of *Plains of Promise*, Alexis Wright's first novel, published in 1997:

> The biggest tree on St Dominic's Mission for Aborigines grew next to the girls' dormitory. It was the only tree that had survived from the twenty-one seeds contained in a seed pod brought by the first missionary on the long and arduous trek to the claypans expanding across the northern Gulf country.

This is how 'God's celebrated poinciana tree' – as Wright puts it, with irony that only hardens over the novel's course – 'came into being, surviving the claypans, the droughts and the Wets to grow large and graceful in the presence of three generations of black girls laughing in their innocence as if nothing mattered at all'.

On one hand, the native gum, felled to make way for that peculiarly modern vision of the Western metropolis; on the other, a 'thirsty, greedy foreign tree intruding into the bowels' of an Indigenous world, putting down roots, gaining in size and vigour as those around it are exploited, suffer loss of culture, weaken or die.

The crucial difference between these openings is that White writes on the other side of the catastrophe that he prophesies. His work bears witness to the historical hurt that resulted from European presence in Australia, just as his guilt at being a beneficiary of that presence was deployed to acknowledge and support those who were disenfranchised by it. He universalised his own sense of outsiderdom, transforming it into the empathetic magic of his fiction. But he could not know the pain of colonisation from the inside, not directly. What makes *Plains of Promise* such a landmark work is that it arrives at the vanguard of fictions that *do*.

This is what makes Alexis's debut so fascinating. In it we watch the author feel her way to a form appropriate to communicating this terrible, yet magnificent, perspective. It's a novel that wavers between a social-realist register of the kind that characterised much twentieth-century literature of protest – a tradition largely inherited from working-class men writing in English – and a mode of narration based on Indigenous lore and oral storytelling culture: multivalent, multivocal and strange. You could say the unevenness of this early work is part of its point. *Plains of Promise* is the novel where Alexis Wright works out what kind of writer she needs to be.

~

All of it begins with a single crow. The native bird comes to perch in the poinciana not long before the suicide of a woman who had lived for a short time in St Dominic's Mission. Her death is one of despair. She had been removed from her people and from her Country; and, once at the mission, her daughter, who is half white, was taken from her and placed in a boarding house with other girls.

We're in the 1950s, in the Gulf country of Queensland's far North. It's the area Alexis Wright's own people were obliged to move to after dispossession by cattle station owners on adjoining territory. But even here, living under the obligatory tenets of Christianity, the men and women of the mission know that the bird is ill-omened in an older sense. Its intermittent returns presage more deaths among their people. And it is Ivy Koopundi, daughter of the suicide, whom many hold responsible for its presence.

Wright's depiction of Ivy's growth to maturity is one of stunning understatement. The girl is rejected and mistrusted by her peers and soon preyed upon by the spiritual and temporal leader of the mission, Errol Jipp, a man with godlike powers of 'protection' granted to him by the Queensland government over the eight hundred or so souls in the mission. Jipp's predations result in Ivy's pregnancy – and, once her daughter is born, following a brutal and lonely labour, that child, too, is removed, one more daughter of the stolen generations.

Those few at the mission who retain knowledge of the complex protocols of their law are disturbed by Ivy's link to the crow, as well as to the deaths that continue to plague the mission. Eventually they conclude that one of their number, a young man named Elliot, must go travelling into the land of Ivy Koopundi's people in search of knowledge.

Once free of the mission's confines, something unprecedented happens to Wright's narrative. It's as if the novel discovers a concomitant freedom to expand, unencumbered by European diktat – and does so by furnishing a thrilling account of

Elliot's journey. Instead of proceeding on terms laid down by the white world, *Plains of Promise* allows itself to unfurl in these pages, alert to its own sense of meaning and worth. Elliot's progress is that of a man attempting to live in proper relation to place; his creator attempts a style that reflects this.

Here he is, having made camp after a difficult march to the edge of Ivy's Country and the shore of a lake reduced to a muddy trickle by drought, in a passage worth quoting at length:

> They came in the stillness of the night. It was the crows that sent up the first noisy alarm. A million squawking birds followed, creating a racket of such intensity it pierced the senses. At first Elliot thought it was just some dingoes he had seen in a small pack earlier in the day, robbing eggs from unguarded nests. He had watched them run off with the rounded eggs, unbroken,

> in their mouths. But now a roaring body created by thousands upon thousands of winged creatures lifting off in unison hid the light of the moon. Elliot imagined it was the Great Spirit troubled into action; he felt a cool change of the quick wind in the air touch his skin in the darkness and thought he was being struck down on the [Rainbow] Serpent's path of destruction.

Here are the first glimmers of Wright's big-sky style: the bringing into concert of meteorology and topography via conjunctions that allow clause upon clause to pile up like clouds in the Wet; the vast animal choruses summoned to populate place; and the supernatural shiver running beneath it all, hinting at some immense, chthonic region of alternative meaning.

It's the mode that Wright will perfect in *Carpentaria* (2006) and *The Swan Book* (2013) – and raise to a shattering crescendo in 2023's

Praiseworthy. But it is also a correlate of sorts to the disturbance that Ivy's exile has caused. Elliot will return to the mission with knowledge that shunts the whole novel off its tracks.

Plains of Promise follows Ivy into a very different Australia than that described on Elliot's journey. The novel's latter sections, which leap forwards years and decades at a time, reveal a society in which the culture-destroying strictures of mission-led religion have been converted into the apparently objective realm of science and the potentially liberatory one of politics.

Yet every supposed improvement in the situation of Indigenous Australians that an unctuous and self-congratulatory cast of white saviours describes in the novel is revealed to be yet another trap, another means of socially engineering poverty and despair. Even when Indigenous political action presents a way forwards, it threatens to exacerbate fractures between urban activists and traditional communities. The roots of the poinciana run deep;

the crows still gather in its branches.

Wright enacts these incommensurable elements on the page by tacking between magical realism (in the case of Ivy, now the long-time inmate of a mental institution) and a more sober realism that colours the experience of Ivy's now-adult daughter, Mary, soon to be a mother herself, who has been raised by white parents but who aches to know her birth family and people.

Having established herself as a sincere and energetic campaigner on Indigenous affairs in the city, Mary is sent back by chance intelligence to the mission country where Ivy started out all those years before. Back at St Dominic's with her daughter, Jessie, in tow, Mary is confronted by the consequences of generations of misgovernment and collective trauma.

Wright's achievement here lies in the unflinching clarity of her vision. This is not to be the home-coming readers might wish for. The old people of the mission have not overcome their mistrust of

Ivy and her progeny; they still fear the evil that shadows them. And the final reconnection of Mary with her mother is partial, ambiguous.

Plains of Promise is a bitterly ironic title for a novel that concludes with so little assurance for the future. The blight of the poinciana tree has spread across the land and touched everything; it is ecological and ontological at once. But however dark Wright's vision, however depleted of hope, this remarkable document reframes the nightmare of Indigenous subjection in the author's terms.

From here on, through a career that has only grown in imaginative power and grace, Wright will fill the *terra nullius* of white Australia with undeniable, indelible descriptions of Indigenous presence. If a place belongs to those who write with fiercest affection for it, this was the point when readers began to dwell on Wright's Country. Think of *Plains of Promise* as the native sapling from which the decolonisation of a continent might grow.

CARPENTARIA

It takes a particular kind of knowledge to go with the river, whatever its mood.

Carpentaria was a novel that almost didn't happen. Two years in conception and six years in the writing, Wright's manuscript was rejected by every major Australian publisher before landing on the desk of Ivor Indyk at Giramondo in the early 2000s. The editorial relationship which began then would become the most significant in contemporary Australian literature.

Indyk was Whitlam Professor at what is now Western Sydney University: a critic, teacher and scholar of daunting intelligence, a deep and idiosyncratic reader. He'd recently left the University of Sydney and from his new base at Parramatta established *HEAT*, a groundbreaking literary magazine, as well as Giramondo, a publisher backed by the university but driven by Indyk's desire to create a fresh cultural outpost in Sydney's demographic heart.

Indyk, the Jewish intellectual outsider; Wright, an Indigenous author with a love of European modernism: an oddly apposite marriage of minds. That the pair worked hard on shaping *Carpentaria* into its final form can perhaps be intuited from the greater length and sense of relatively minimal editorial intervention that marks *Praiseworthy* (think of *Ulysses* as against *Finnegans Wake*). Whatever the exact nature of their collaboration, the result was a novel of the kind that *Plains of Promise* only hinted at: epic in scale, formally experimental, defiantly written from an Indigenous perspective.

Carpentaria proved to be a literary hinge. In 1938, Xavier Herbert's *Capricornia* (a work whose title and subject matter are echoed and subverted in Wright's work) introduced Australia's Top End into the nation's literary imagination. Almost four decades later, Helen Garner's 1977 debut *Monkey*

Grip shifted readers' attention to urban experience and evolving social and sexual mores.

On its publication in 2006, *Carpentaria* flipped the table. There had never been anything like it. It went on to win the Miles Franklin Award (Wright becoming the first Indigenous author to win the prize outright), the ALS Gold Medal and the Queensland and Victorian premier's literary awards for fiction. It was reviewed in terms that mingled admiration, perplexity and simple awe. Yet on the day Wright was awarded the Miles Franklin, Australia's pre-eminent literary honour, then prime minister John Howard announced a suite of measures tightening white control over Indigenous communities known as the Intervention.

~

How should we think about the unique aspects of *Carpentaria*? Where others might have lingered over the obvious misery of Indigenous fringe dwellers in 'Desperance', where the novel is set – torn from ancestral lands and dumped on the outskirts of a white township, a place run by shallow and venal men who hold the black population in contempt – Wright instead does something unexpected: she renders her cast as mock heroic figures, like something out of an eighteenth-century Menippean satire by Jonathan Swift. (It's worth noting that *Gulliver's Travels* often takes the titular character to Australia, or a version of it; Swift was a close reader of William Dampier's *Voyages*.)

Menippean satire is a (mainly) prose form of satire in which ideas and attitudes, rather than peoples and places, are mocked. It contains elements of allegory, the picaresque and pure satire. When we first meet the character Angel Day, for example, clutching a blessed virgin sculpture with a clock embedded in it, treasure looted from the town tip, the gap between her activities as a scavenger and haughty pride at her find is a matter for sharp commentary on her neighbours' part.

But Wright does not set her creation up for simple laughs.

Instead, Angel – and her husband, Normal Phantom, and the novel's Indigenous cast of characters – are granted freedom by the satirical eye cast over them, while figures such as Bruiser, the racist town mayor, are diminished by the same perspective. The 'Pricklebush' people to whom Angel and Normal belong are deeply in earnest, yes – yet they are far from earnest.

Wright grants them the nobility of humour: a sort of clowning shields the seriousness and dignity of a deeper personhood. She shows that while these folk are looked down upon by the mostly white population of 'Uptown', locked in conflict with the non-traditional owners and Indigenous chancers of the 'Eastside' mob, residents of the town's other encampment, they remain carriers of immemorial law.

The 'Uptown' folk, by contrast, have forgotten their own religion, clinging instead to the fragile superiority garnered from land theft a few generations deep – while the Eastside crew will act against Country for economic gain. Here a refined literary method ennobles simple folk with complex natures while condemning their would-be racial superiors and Indigenous competitors in a way that is wholly new.

Then there is the rhythm of Wright's prose. *Plains of Promise* tacks, back and forth, between registers that sit together uneasily: the smooth, tidy, official sentences of standard-issue realism and the more expansive, circular and circuitous rhythms that indicate Indigenous perspective.

Carpentaria merges these registers in ways that ironise the limited perspective traditional Anglo realism brings to bear on Australian place. Wright folds that realism into the larger rhythms of her paragraphs. Her maximalist style, which incorporates suddenly shifting narrative perspectives and tonal changes, is actually based on a minimalist approach: patterns of repetition, for example –

phrases modulated slightly, then reused; a constant rolling tempo in which subtle syncopation disturbs the potential for monotony; and a kind of semantic drone, in which words, phrases, sentences do not line up obediently to furnish meaning but, rather, establish a series of consonances.

Strict sense or meaning, then, is subordinate in *Carpentaria*'s pages to the generation of a total environment. Wright's style is shaped by landscape, conforms itself to Country – it's language as an instance of echolocation, not imposition of words over place. If we wanted to get fancy about it, we might say that her words *enact* a form of imaginative decolonisation.

~

The novel opens with the estrangement of Normal Phantom – a droll, determined river-dwelling elder – from his devout wife, Angel Day. Will Phantom, their son, has fled Desperance after clashing with both the mining company set to commence operations near town and more conservative Aboriginal factions. Indeed, the whole of Desperance is divided – racially, ideologically and spiritually – between the offspring of white settlers, Indigenous groups and corporate interests.

When the Gurfurritt company starts mining on sacred land, those tensions are inflamed. Norm Phantom's resistance, quietly effective, contrasts with the Eastside mob's complicity with the company under the leadership of Joseph Midnight. Meanwhile, Will Phantom eventually joins his father in acts of resistance to the environmental despoliation brought about by the mine's operations, having undergone profound changes while following the magnetic, prophet-like Mozzie Fishman and a band of Indigenous men on a journey of ancestral renewal.

Will Phantom's return to Desperance threatens an uneasy balance of power. The acts of resistance he and his father coordinate escalate the conflict. Angel, however, trapped between faith and despair, is driven by the same events to mental breakdown.

But a SparkNotes outline of *Carpentaria*'s narrative only takes us so far. Angel's distress is not only psychological. Any novel limited to describing the interior mental states of a secular individual can only catch a portion of what Wright is attempting to describe here – a total psychic disintegration whose most significant aspect is its spiritual cast.

Angel's hurt stems from the way her cherished beliefs are Biblical tales (as Mozzie Fishman puts it) 'that lived in someone else's desert':

> Angel Day now lived on the very outer reaches of the family. She was estranged from everyone – her husband, her children, the neighbours, the town. She had gone mad with talking to God. People said she was always talking to herself, singing hymns at all hours of the day and night, disturbing

> the dogs who howled in fright. Her shack was falling to bits, but she would not move. She lived surrounded by pictures of Jesus and Mary, her walls dripping with crucifixes, bibles, and pages torn from prayer books stuck with dried flour paste. She fasted. She scoured her flesh with steel wool. She made loud confessions of her sins to no one. And all the while, she said the Lord was watching over her. She said He was coming to take her home. They said, poor old Angel, she's just another crazy old black woman talking to ghosts.

Likewise, Will Phantom's journey of transformation is not merely personal – some shallow act of contemporary self-actualisation – but an ontological sea change that leaves him a spiritual warrior more than rebellious youth or political activist:

> He became the spirit man, the man who walked with the ancestors. The man who knew things the government could not control. The man who went to the place where the bones were singing.

The novel's climax is, then, appropriately, one in which a spiritually animated climacteric brings destruction – a narrative co-production of myth and ecology that dismantles already shaky boundaries between Western and Indigenous realities. Desperance, always a frail, contingent outpost in hostile Country, suffers a physical unravelling to rival its moral reckoning.

Ending is the hardest thing for fiction to accomplish, since it is at once the most satisfying function of literature – to give a sense of completion to a reality which is in fact open-ended and chaotic – and the part of any story that feels most artificially imposed. Wright's sense of an ending is not that of the novel, at least the realist kind, but of the poem whose conclusion is a return to beginnings.

Carpentaria is an epic of return, whether to land or law or spirit. The novel's characters do not die, or marry, or sail off to other lands so much as they slip out of the quondam realism of Desperance and white Australia, more broadly conceived, into the ancestral realm. This realm is one Wright accesses through the imagination and describes in fictional terms, but it takes on an increasingly independent existence. Here, for the first time – though not nearly the last – Wright's creations embrace a sovereignty disallowed them elsewhere.

There is a final tension, of course. What change can a merely imaginative act – a novel, even one as passionate and persuasive as *Carpentaria* – effect upon the world it seeks to describe and critique? Surely the trade-off for the pure creative freedom the author enjoys is political impotence in the 'real' world, the Australia of the neo-European settler-colonial project – the world in which we live?

In the course of writing this book I had the opportunity to read English writer Robert Macfarlane's *Is a River Alive?* It is a work written partly in dialogue with Alexis Wright – indeed, lines by Alexis form the epigraph to one of its chapters. The pair have been friends via email for years.

Macfarlane's first chapter describes events that took place in the months after the publication of *Carpentaria* – the drafting of a new constitution in Ecuador, a successful vote for which took place after a night when the nation's lawmakers gave the parliament over to indigenous peoples to perform certain rites in its chamber, invoking the presence of ancestral spirits to guide the hands of mundane politicians.

Macfarlane, drawing on the ideas of First Nation thinkers in Canada, sees this moment as a 'binocular' one, in which an indigenous lens was joined with contemporary political and legal structures to enact potentially radical change: enshrining, for the first time anywhere in the world, 'rights of nature' in a nation's constitutional order.

This meant that later, when Canadian and Australian miners sought to establish gold and copper mines near a river in the cloud forests of Northern Ecuador – one of the most pristine and richly biodiverse ecosystems on Earth – that river was granted standing as a living entity in the eyes of the courts.

In the late 2010s, these mines were blocked by those same courts. Los Cedros was protected from the toxic by-products of mines polluting its waters. It was the first victory against extractive industries by the rights-of-nature movement. Earlier this year, Mount Taranaki in New Zealand became the third mountain in that country to be granted 'legal personhood' in the eyes of the law.

These are concrete changes with real-world consequences. And they are shifts driven by the imaginative efforts of indigenous people worldwide to provide a scaffolding in which others may come to understand their vision of the world – and agitate, alongside them, for changes in contemporary politics and law that reflect that vision.

In moments such as these, *Carpentaria*'s opening, with its description of the Rainbow Serpent's continuing presence in the river delta of the Gulf, suddenly takes on a renewed force. Wright is not some backwater isolate, fighting a hopeless, rearguard action in defence of a way of thinking and a way of life destined for extinction. She is at the forefront of a global effort to reimagine our compact with the natural world.

THE SWAN BOOK

Eight years after the birth of Christ, the Roman poet Ovid was banished to the Black Sea port of Tomis, having inadvertently offended Emperor

Augustus with some verses in praise of adultery. The poetry Ovid composed in exile was very different from the urbane eroticism of his years of metropolitan success. It was the work of a man who considered himself buried alive. It reeked of sadness, isolation, pride, self-pity and anger.

His *Ibis*, for example, modelled on an earlier piece by Callimachus, is what Latin scholars call an elegiac curse-poem. Its running catalogue of mythical tales was designed to reflect changing facets of the poet's inner despair. Yet Ovid's summoning of these mythological figures had an extraliterary aim: supernatural payback against those who caused the poet's banishment.

Consciously or not, *The Swan Book*, first published in 2013 – a much-anticipated follow-up to Wright's multi-award-winning *Carpentaria* – is also a curse-poem. Like *Ibis* it emerges from the experience of exile: in this case, the physical displacement and inward migration of Indigenous Australians since European arrival in 1788. It also employs myths drawn from Aboriginal and Western sources as a way of making universal the phenomenon of banishment, whether from country, language or traditional law. The fantastical shifts in each work are outward expressions of the effects of psychological isolation over time. But if Ovid's poems of exile promise redemption through the simple exercise of verse-making – restoration won through persistent creative effort – Alexis Wright's third novel offers no consolation, only anathema.

Set during an unspecified moment in near-future Australia, *The Swan Book* describes a country irreparably altered by the effects of climate change but still mired in the stale politics of racial paternalism. Ongoing military intervention has left some Indigenous communities transformed into de facto prisons, while others, having inveigled themselves into the good graces of the governing elite, win funding to integrate younger generations into the white mainstream. The wider world has suffered social disturbance of the kind we associate with wartime: civil strife, mass exodus, reversion to tribal violence. All that touches the lives of these fringe dwellers in their geographic remove, however, is palls of desert sand and drought dust, occasionally tamped down by flood.

Oblivion Ethyl(ene) – Oblivia – lives in an Indigenous swamp encampment surrounded by government razor wire, in the iron hull of an abandoned navy craft. As a child she was discovered huddled among the roots of a eucalypt by the sole white woman in the community, a European émigré named Bella Donna. Oblivia is mute, silenced by the early trauma of gang-rape, but Bella Donna is the garrulous carrier of Old World lore. This boat person from the Global North bequeaths to Ethyl an obsession with swans and the human stories that have grown up around them. Soon the majestic birds start to congregate on the swamp, drawn somehow to the voiceless girl.

Another drawn to Oblivia is Warren Finch, a local boy made good. Finch was the talented child of government largesse, an Indigenous leader in the making. But his political rise to deputy president of the nation has come at the cost of connection to his people. It is his return to the swamp in adulthood to abduct Oblivia as his 'promise-bride' that sets the plot – if, indeed, the sequence of events the novel describes can be given such a basic label – in motion.

Because *The Swan Book* is both animated and wounded by the intensity of its retributive message, it is a work in which passages of striking prose interrupt others of determined descriptive weirdness, as if the author discovered that despite her facility with the conqueror's language, it was unsuited to the world she wished to portray.

In isolation, then, a paragraph such as the following has a sinuous beauty. It makes poetry from an aggregation of clauses that rise barometrically, a phenomenon made of both myth and meteorology:

A low-pressure weather system was unpredictable and nobody knew whether it would bring more dry storms or blue skies sulking through another year. Still, a flood of mythical proportions would be required to drive the sand back into the sea. The ceremonies sang on and on for majestic ancestral spirits to turn up out of the blue, to stir up the atmospheric pressure with their breath, to turn the skies black with themselves, to create such a deluge to unplug the swamp, to take the sand mountain back to the sea. The ancestral sand spirits flew like a desert storm and backed themselves even further up the mountain. Silt gathering in the swamp lapped against the dwellings of the increasing population and crept further inwards as the swamp decreased in size. This was the new story written in scrolls of intricate lacework formed by the salt crystals that the drought left behind.

Joined together over the course of more than three hundred pages, Wright's mashup of sing-song fabulism and political invective, first-person perspective and omniscient narration, ancient myth and popular culture threatens to overwhelm readers. The trembling realism of *Plains of Promise* is long gone, transformed via the epic chant that is *Carpentaria*; we're wholly inside Wright's mature style in these pages.

We also find the narrative norms of the Western novel have been jettisoned. Where most instances of the contemporary apocalyptic, from Cormac McCarthy's *The Road* to HBO's *The Last of Us*, use atomic warfare or pandemic or some associated calamity to depopulate the world, the better to strain out pure sounds of human interaction from the white noise of technological modernity, Wright's work packs more life than ever into its account of a future Australia. *The Swan Book* is a veritable ark of collective nouns: plagues of rats, parliaments of owls, flights of butterflies and clouds of locusts all battle for descriptive attention in a continent whose weather patterns have been inverted, drying the fertile fringes and drowning the land's arid heart. These animal invasions are the indicators of a place where the immemorial natural order has been upset.

This feral ecosystem has correspondences in the social realm, too. Climate change has inundated the cities of the east coast, destroying the economy and forcing entire populations into exodus. Little in the way of settled culture survives, except among the rich and politically powerful like Warren Finch. Such is the gap between the haves and have-nots in this world that the wasteful extravagance of the one-percenters seems all the more obscene, as when Oblivia is obliged to attend a feast:

> The tables were festooned with red fish, octopus, squid, oysters and silver urns overflowing with prawns, crayfish, salmon and

> other things cooked red from the sea. A line of waiters queued at the door with platters of steaming roasts and vegetables under shining silver lids. It was a banquet, more food than the girl had seen in her entire life, and the sight of so much food made her nauseous, and unable to eat. Inside her loneliness, she felt the pangs of hunger the night she had raided the fishing nests in the swamp, and had not found a single fish. Then, she lost track of the number of cattle, pigs, sheep and poultry slaughtered, and vegetable fields that had been raided, the sea emptied, and all of this – deteriorating into the guts of seagulls eating the rubbish.

So, the imagination that impels *The Swan Book* is of uncommon extremity. It makes the novels of Thomas Pynchon read like those of Anthony Trollope. Yet these chaotic, hallucinatory procedures come to possess their own logic and cumulative power. Collectively they represent the fictional equivalent of Wright's celebrated speech in response to the Howard government's Northern Territory Intervention of 2007 – an attack on the existing social, racial and political order of the Australian present, couched in fabulous and futuristic terms.

You could even say that the literary success of *The Swan Book* is a corollary to the political failures that Wright and her generation of activists have suffered. From the Yirrkala Bark Petitions of 1963 to the Uluru Statement from the Heart, first shared in 2017, numerous public interventions were mounted by Indigenous Australians seeking acknowledgment of their unique presence and the satisfaction of their specific needs.

We know how mixed the success of these efforts has been. While the richness and venerability of Indigenous peoples in Australia have been recognised in limited and symbolic terms, political agency has remained stubbornly out of reach.

Wright, along with her peers, was an eloquent voice in seeking Indigenous answers to Indigenous issues: to do otherwise, from her perspective, was to be obliged into the kind of assimilative outcomes that had already caused so much injury.

From early non-fiction works by Wright, such as 1997's *Grog War* and the many essays and editorials and speeches penned by her in the years since, a certain orientation towards power was evinced: if white Australians listened, and listened hard, to what black Australians were saying – about sovereignty, or the unique approaches to, say, law or social organisation that their people possessed and needed to deploy in order to recover agency and self-respect – then rapprochement of some kind was possible.

Wright's novels are not so confident. Increasingly they become the zone where disenchantment with the course and speed of political change can be performed imaginatively, with a freedom denied elsewhere. *The Swan Book* is a kind of fulcrum in this shift. It's the work in which the ideological efforts that informed so much of Wright's public activism go underground. From now on, Wright's vision of a supernatural world drawn from Indigenous lore – one coterminous with the official, rational world imposed by colonial fiat – would serve as the creative repository for ideas that were truly revolutionary. It would be her works of fiction – stories to which the powers that be were indifferent – that would furnish the possibility of a more profound method of insurrection.

Viewed this way, *The Swan Book*'s manic incoherence assumes a paradoxical lucidity. The Viennese writer and satirist Karl Kraus believed that if we were truly able to imagine the reality behind the dry data in our morning newspapers, then the world, in its collective horror, would be obliged to change that reality. As the scholar Erich Heller says, 'if one man's imagination were inspired by it and gave expression to it, all the tragedies of ancient Greece would dwindle into idyllic sentimentalities before such a drama of human corruption and human agony.'

Wright attempts in *The Swan Book* to give expression, though a multiplicity of stories and voices, to the historical disaster visited upon Aboriginal Australia. Her effort was designed to close the gap between authentic existence and collective imagination, a black intervention into white Australians' complacent mentality. As Oblivia, now a princess trapped in a tower, suggests, 'even true stories have to be invented sometimes to be remembered.'

For all its confusions and longueurs, its cynicism and bitterness, *The Swan Book* should be regarded as one of the most beautiful, furious and urgent novels to be published in this country in recent years. It reminds readers that the misery and upheaval promised by climate change have already come to Australia's First Peoples. Their exile is not a story from our distant past, in other words, but a harbinger of our collective future.

TRACKER

Leigh Bruce 'Tracker' Tilmouth was one of those figures, so much larger than life, that only the immense spaces of the Top End could accommodate. The story of his early years was tragically common for its era. It should have done him in – left him broken in spirit, as it destroyed so many of his generation – but he exceeded his circumstances and used them as rocket fuel, powering a can-do activism that was equal parts bush politics and serial entrepreneurship.

Tracker was born an Eastern Arrernte man in 1954 and spent his early years in Alice Springs. His mother died when he was still a young boy, and while an aunt and uncle sought to adopt him, welfare authorities decided that he and his two younger brothers, the 'dark ones' of the eight siblings, should be sent north: first to Darwin and a notorious children's home, then to the mission on Croker Island, where they spent the next decade, the brothers unaware that they had other siblings.

He was luckier than many others in the Stolen Generations. He had some family with him, an idyllic, wild, if fairly rustic, home and a fair-minded, devout housemother who tried to awaken in the children some sense of their circumstances by reading them novels such as Alan Paton's apartheid-era *Cry, the Beloved Country*.

Sent back to Darwin for his education, Bruce Tilmouth showed himself to be precociously clever and defiantly ill-adjusted for school. He dropped out young, worked in an abattoir and became involved in petty crime before being sent to Angas Downs Station, an Indigenous-owned property, where he was taken in by people connected with his birth family. There he divided his days between reclaiming traditional culture and the dusty business of running and maintaining a working station.

He remained a joker and an annoyance to more stolid co-workers there, but a seriousness of purpose crept in. The arrival of the Whitlam government and the good offices of Charlie Perkins opened Tracker's horizons. He studied environmental science and natural resource management at Roseworthy College and, in his own words, 'got some letters after my name'.

The latter part of Tracker's life and career is part of the public record. Among numerous roles, he was director of the Central Land Council, which represented Aboriginal people in an area more than ten times the size of Tasmania. He helped establish the Central Australian Aboriginal Legal Aid Service, as well as the region's Aboriginal health service, and was frontrunner for preselection for the ALP's NT Senate seat before dropping out of contention.

Prior to his early death from cancer and heart problems at sixty-two, Tracker placed his considerable energies, political nous and generosity of spirit in the service of advancement for Indigenous Australians. He had no time for passive welfare programs and believed that a vibrant Indigenous economy was the basis for cultural rejuvenation and political power. This position, combined with a take-no-prisoners approach to negotiations with white politicians and other Indigenous movers and shakers, made him a figure of ambivalence – he infuriated as many as he charmed – but few gainsaid his intelligence and vision.

~

Such is the front office account of Tracker Tilmouth's life and achievements. And yet, great complexity underlies the transmission of Indigenous experience via Western literary genres of 'life writing'.

'A western style biography would never do,' wrote Alexis Wright in her introduction to *Tracker*:

> It would not have been a wise move for any biographer, or the correct way to attempt to remember somebody like Tracker, who

tried with just about every breath he drew
to manufacture enormous change.

This was an argument drawn from her long personal friendship with the man. Alexis regarded him, indeed, with a certain awe. He was someone who sought 'to sculpt land, country and people into a brilliant future on a grand scale'. He was 'a statesman for dreams that were much bigger and better than the realities he saw around him'.

But there is a broader critique embedded in her approach to the project. The idea of a human existence described in terms bracketed off from other selves – that rich matrix of family, community and wider society so important to First Nations culture – is a European invention dating mainly from the Romantic era.

Romantic autobiography is built on the political auto-inventions of Napoleon, the solitary metaphysics of Rousseau, the literary performances of Wordsworth, Chateaubriand, De Quincey and others – all of them concerned with prismatic shifts in individual consciousness over time.

Romanticism is often characterised by another notion that renders it alien to Aboriginal philosophy and worldview. It regards humans as divorced from, even actively fighting against, nature. As the historian of ideas Isaiah Berlin, writing about the German playwright Schiller, put it:

> he makes a vast contrast between nature, which [is] elemental, capricious ... and man, who has morality, who distinguishes between desire and will, duty and interest, the right and the wrong, and acts accordingly, if need be against nature.

So, autobiography in its Western forms may be problematic when it comes to recording Indigenous lives. Yet Tracker regarded life writing as a necessity – 'I want you to write something for me, Wrighty,' he told his putative biographer.

He understood, for example, that to be treated as a citizen of a democracy one must first be regarded as a person deserving of citizenship. Telling the story of the self becomes a precondition for political agency.

And there is a further layer of obligation: to recover what was lost over two centuries of forced displacement, exterminatory efforts and assimilationist policy. There is an existential duty to assemble and verify those narratives of selfhood which survive these eras. Moreover, engendering that sense of pride and community – the basis for survival for any embattled culture – also requires heroes and heroines, stories of conflict and reconciliation, models of probity, decency, outrage or wisdom to admire and emulate.

Life writing is, then, an awkward undertaking for those who would otherwise prioritise communal identity over an individuated one. But those of us who are latecomers to this continent should be grateful that this awkwardness is overcome.

Life writing from Indigenous perspectives offers the rest of us an opportunity to meet, recognise and empathise with experiences very different to our own.

~

Alexis Wright impaled herself on the horns of this dilemma in *Tracker*. She didn't merely assemble a posthumous autobiography as an editor might, even though Tracker's own words and recollections make up a good chunk of the total in its pages. Nor did she produce a biography, strictly speaking, since there is no obvious commanding intelligence here, filtering the multiple voices it contains, imposing a singular vision of his life through selection, interpretation, expansion or elision of people, places and events.

What Wright produced instead was a 'collective memoir': an account of Tracker's life and work told through the voices of those who knew him. It's a democratic undertaking (though before his death Tracker chose those voices he wished to speak) with a strong tang of oral tradition, even on the page. Its dominant mode is the yarn – the tale whose point is in the telling – and the tone is laconic throughout. A lack of sentimentality is evident, even in the description of terrible events or circumstances; more often there is the anarchic energy of those who have nothing to lose.

The total effect of *Tracker* is one of narrative imbrication: stories overlapping one another like scales of snakeskin. One person's perspective of an event is bolstered, enlarged, undercut or illuminated by another. The effect can be slyly comic, or else it can burrow deep into some private grief. The multiplicity of perspectives can be exhausting – you could think of it as 'slow' biography, sharing with slow cinema a relaxed approach to plot and an affection for long, unbroken takes – but it is also a form that manages to encompass the communal experience of Indigenous Australia while celebrating a visionary individual.

What Wright achieved in *Tracker* is a considerable literary workaround. She found a method that enacts the complex relationship between self and community that a Western biography cannot – she created a work that understands that the individual only becomes explicable in relation to the group. Though *Tracker* is a book shaped to Bruce Tilmouth's unique personality and situation, caught as he was between traditional culture and the social and political demands of the present, its final effect – it is at first raucously noisy, but then the repetitions, backtrackings, digressions gather and burgeon – has a magnificent choral quality. As Alexis explains:

> [I]t takes the voices of many to tell the stories of country, the story lines. This is because stories are powerful and must be handled carefully, as when they are sung by many men and women from their parts of the long song travelling over country. Each

should speak for themselves, and for the whole to form the consensus, or complete story. This is how it goes for our responsibility to country, ourselves, and for our times, as the carriers of all time.

PRAISEWORTHY

It's hard to know quite how to approach *Praiseworthy*. This is a novel so outsized, after all – so maximal in its aesthetic, so fierce in its denunciation of our nation's failed politics and our world's self-destructive propensities – that initially it feels forbidding, even frankly absurd. To open its pages is to jump onto a spinning carousel: a blinding dazzle of light, sound and colour, with a teeming equine mob set to mechanical gallop.

Yet it is simultaneously a work of stillness and poise. Little actually happens in narrative terms for a book so large. Some of the novel's central figures barely move over the course of hundreds of pages. The world may dance busily about them, but they remain almost stationary. They partake of the eternal, these characters; they're half embedded in another realm. For all the tragedy of their daily existences, the dereliction of their home, the poisoning of their environment, there is grandeur to the attitudes they hold. They have, at best, exceeded the bounds of a reality imposed upon them.

And what form does this reality take? An Indigenous township named Praiseworthy, somewhere in the Gulf Country of Queensland's Far North, begins to suffer from a haze of choking red dust – a pall that settles over the town and will not shift. Many residents regard the dust dome as the work of ancestral spirits. But one senior local – called Widespread, though he has other names – determines this is climate change made manifest.

In light of this understanding, Widespread hatches a plan. He sets out to muster dozens, then hundreds, then thousands of feral donkeys.

(It's worth noting that Tracker Tilmouth was called Donkey by Wright; I suspect something of Tracker's energy and visionary pitch is lent to Widespread here.) He claims these hardy creatures will be the engines of a hugely profitable 'sustainable transport conglomerate' once the age of fossil fuels is played out, though for now they mill in the streets, much to the displeasure of his neighbours and estranged wife, Dance, who carries her own exquisite menagerie – great clouds of moths and butterflies – wherever she goes.

When Widespread and Dance's eldest son disappears, having perhaps committed suicide in the waters of the Gulf, his family and the townspeople are grief-stricken. Everyone aside from the missing young man's brother, Tommyhawk, a child so indoctrinated by online modernity and a lurid tabloid press that he's convinced all the males of the town are paedophiles. He wants his missing brother jailed for sleeping with an underage girl. He dreams that the nation's prime minister will adopt him and take him back to Canberra, the heart of white Australia.

Tommyhawk is not alone. The town mayor, Ice Pick, wants the residents of Praiseworthy to assimilate more completely into mainstream Australian life. Soon Maximum Security, a hulking cop from the south, arrives in Praiseworthy, in search of sexual predators and bearing his own disturbing ideas about racial purity.

As these characters flicker in and out of narrative focus, weird occurrence piles on. Elements of ancestral myth bleed into the town's contemporary reality, just as obligations to old lore bump up against the necessity of economic self-determination. The kitchen-sink drama of Indigenous life in the town, with its feuds and cliques and rumour mills (all related in pungent vernacular), is interrupted by passages tuned, with delicacy and power, to the natural world and those members of the community who remain alert to it.

Like its predecessors, *Praiseworthy* does not

resolve into a novel in the traditional sense. Even granting the wildness of *The Swan Book*, this is a work of extraordinary unruliness. Think of it as an ecology in its totality rendered sensate: a novel in which a whalebone skeleton or a dust-storm 'speaks' on equal footing with human characters; a narrative, moreover, in which profane 'Western' time clashes with the endless now of the sacred and where imported notions of individual human agency are dissolved in a collective 'we'. Here Wright takes the cumulative fervour of her political activism and her depthless cultural endowment – the most venerable archive of story the world has known – and blends it using the cyclonic force of her imagination.

I've written before of the ways in which Wright uses the real-world situation of black Australia to animate her fiction. *Praiseworthy* may appear to centre on a single township and one dysfunctional family who dwell there, but this is a novel that contains the total horizon of

Indigenous experience. The terrible repercussions of genocide and then assimilation, the ongoing racism directed toward Indigenous communities, the economic deprivation, the sundered families: all of it figures in these pages. Not for nothing is the beloved, broken, missing son of Widespread and Dance named 'Aboriginal Sovereignty'.

Indeed, the sheer scale of *Praiseworthy*, the wildness of its stylistic shifts, the adamancy of its rhetoric, doesn't distinguish the novel from its predecessors so much as bind it to them more tightly. It reveals fresh layers of significance in those earlier works. We might best regard *Praiseworthy* as the most assertive addition yet to a single, quarter-century-long Aboriginal epic. The same manic digressiveness and determinedly illogical cast, interrupted by the same passages of transcendent grace and wisdom – only supersaturated. It marks the apogee of Wright's unique and hallucinatory style: one that has surely earned its own designation. Let's call it 'Indigenous realism'.

Here, though, even the most dedicated reader may blanch at the effort the book demands. Why must the novel engage in such excess? Why the palls of dust, why the eclipses of moths, why the herds of donkeys? I've struggled as much as anyone else with this question, though my own childhood in country Australia furnishes some clues.

What Wright ventures is to do justice to the terrible rupture in cultural DNA suffered by First Nations people since European arrival in Australia: the loss of language, lore and connection to country. Her method is to fill those gaps with pseudogenes and viruses and sundry junk; a bulking out that, in its avidity and extremism, results in a literary form that replicates the madness and despair that accompanies dispossession, individual grief and collective loss. Wright's fictions whoomph into this vacuum of human despair.

The feral donkeys that mill across *Praiseworthy*'s pages are the contemporary totem of

Widespread's ambition. First introduced to Australia in the 1860s because, apparently, horses sickened from eating native vegetation, donkeys proved to be as successful as camels at adapting to local conditions. Estimates now run to over five million spread across the continent's arid interior. Some experts believe their grazing benignly maps onto the niche occupied by extinct native herbivores; others regard them as damaging pests. But as exemplars of the unforeseen repercussions of European presence in Australia, they are unavoidably manifest.

Ferality is a dominant, if intermittent, ecological fact of rural and outback Australia, though it is one barely noted in those urban settings where most of us live. Over five decades in country New South Wales, I've lived through two mouse plagues, one rabbit plague and several locust plagues of varying severity. That Wright should draw on similar experiences for her work indicates not a deviation from realism but, instead, a heightened sense of her adjacent reality. But this concentration on animality – obsessively notated in all her novels – has a further, subversive implication.

Among the Wotjobaluk people of Victoria's Wimmera region, invading pastoralists and their shepherds were known as 'people of the sheep' and their totem as Jesus Christ. *The Lamb Enters the Dreaming* was the lovely title of Robert Kenny's 2007 book about the first contact of black and white worlds in this region. Note that it is the animal who enters the Dreaming first.

Sheep and cattle were more significant harbingers of European presence than the whites as they made their way ever deeper into Australian space in numbers infinitely greater than the skeleton crew of white men who tended to them. These animals were more amenable to accommodation by the Indigenous imaginary; they were food sources too. Ever pragmatic, Indigenous Australians welcomed these animals and incorporated them into lore and daily life.

Europeans, by contrast, for all the seismic impact of their arrival, did not make as much of an impression. There is a scene, early on in Mudrooroo Nyoongah's historical novel from 1983, *Doctor Wooreddy's Prescription for Enduring the End of the World*, when a white man in Van Diemen's Land is observed from the perspective of a Nuenonne man from Bruny Island. He is pictured as something closer to a ghost than a person: pale, trapped in constricting garments, flailing through antipodean space as if through a fog. Think of how rarely positive European characters appear in Alexis Wright's fiction. (Belladonna from *The Swan Book* is framed as a later migrant, not a white Australian.) Could it be that Wright's characters regard white people as Doctor Wooreddy regarded that colonist: as sad, angry, addled spirits, deracinated and exiled, lost in a miasma of greed and viciousness of their own making?

Such spiritual sickness on the part of Europeans was presumably appreciated early on by the first Australians. They likely pitied them before hating them for the destruction they wrought. How striking it is, all these years later, to read Wright's words and appreciate that the animals Europeans introduced still have more heft and worth in the eyes of Indigenous Australians. How humbling a demotion: as if all the hurt they have brought to bear doesn't even rise to the level of conscious agency. To read *Praiseworthy* – carefully, with open eyes – is to understand that we latecomers have not yet earned full standing. We have merely covered ourselves in disgrace.

This is not to suggest that there is some separatist impulse at work in *Praiseworthy*. Wright's novel is written in English and widely translated, published globally by storied independent publishers and intended for a broad audience of readers. Yet the ways in which the author directs her concentration is considered, and it is telling.

And while white Australia is kept at a distance in the novel's pages, the wounds suffered because of European presence are clear, painful and enduring.

Praiseworthy, indeed, is a fiction doubly haunted – first by the loss of the old people who possessed culture and dwelled in easy intimacy with Country, and secondly by the imminent cataclysm of human-induced climate change that threatens those who remain. How, the novel asks, over and over, are we to find that spectrum of belonging 'to all existence' that provided stability to human culture in Australia pre-1788, before the age of 'progress' inaugurated by European arrival helped bring about global disaster. Or, in the townsfolk of *Praiseworthy*'s formulation: 'how to stop dead time from progressing forward' until they have a chance to live, once more, 'inside infinity'.

POSTSCRIPT

In the final weeks of writing this book, my father, who had been dying slowly for more than a decade from non-Hodgkin lymphoma, began dying very fast. As his decline became evident, my mother asked if I would fly up from Tasmania, where I live, and mind the family farm so she could be by his side at a Sydney hospital's oncology unit. These pages were written on much the same patch of Wiradjuri Country in New South Wales that my family has lived on for fifty years.

It's a beautiful place, about a thirty-minute drive south from the town of Orange – undulant, with regular shade trees scattered across paddocks that become densely wooded towards the ridgelines – though once again the region is slipping into drought, pasture bleached and thinning.

Dawn and dusk I mixed feed for the horses and put out round bales for a paddock of bellowing steers. Looking about, with Alexis's words in my head, I felt the landscape to be a visible manifestation of the present – and yet also one in which the past was recorded and stored, like grooves on an LP. It's a notion shared by Wright and Patrick White both: though which pasts, exactly, one is able to access depends on our starting perspective.

White believed, for example, that sites where some atrocity had occurred held some lingering trace of it. Kate Grenville, in the conclusion of *Unsettled*, her 2025 work of non-fiction, describes perceiving this when she stood at the site of the Myall Creek massacre:

> The place itself is the memorial: the ground itself, the actual hills and valleys and rocks and trees and streams of water where the past happened. The truth is right here, right in front of our eyes, still written on the landscape. We just have to look.

My father didn't see it in those terms. He arrived as a young Scottish migrant in the mid-1960s, a teenaged jackeroo sent out briefly to work for one of Australia's old pastoral concerns. Much to his parents' dismay, he stayed on to farm here ever after. His attitude towards Indigenous Australians, as far as I could tell, was a mix of admiration (for the black stockmen he worked with at the beginning of his time in Australia) and inherited racial paternalism. The charity of which he was patron gave grants to young Indigenous men to become contract shearers or fencers, not future leaders. I suspect the only country he saw was that altered by European hands.

There was another reason behind this constricted view. My Scottish father was a runaway from true privilege and inherited wealth: heir to a barony and so a seat in the House of Lords. He was also an Old Etonian and a troubled youngster with parents who thought a year of hard work in the outback would make a man of him. But in that time he escaped the clutches of class and obligation and met my Australian mother, whom he would eventually marry. Thereafter he would seldom return to his ancestral home.

My father rarely spoke about his background, but my brother and I nonetheless grew up with some inkling. Both of us would later move to the UK and discover more. We learned that our family had built a proto-multinational, based primarily in South and North America but with tentacles across the globe. And it had risen to economic and later political power during the nineteenth and twentieth centuries by exploiting the lands and resources of others.

Nitrates from Chile. Grain from the Pacific Northwest. Railways in Argentina. A fleet of ships out of Liverpool. I once told an academic from Peru that my family firm had been involved in early petroleum exploitation in California and Latin America – that we'd owned the Los Lobitos oilfields in Peru. 'We're familiar with

Los Lobitos,' he replied, drily. 'The day they were nationalised is a holiday in our country.'

Our merchant house, Balfour Williamson (though it had many subsidiaries and sister houses), never owned agricultural land in Australia. But the Vesteys' house did. Baron Vestey and Baron Forres – my own family title – were ennobled in the same year. My father and Sam Vestey, the third baron, had been at school together. In our home growing up, Lord Vestey was not the thundering demon of Kev Carmody and Paul Kelly's song; he was one of the gang.

There was one family concern of ours comparable to the Vesteys', albeit modest in scale compared with their holdings in the Top End, and that was Easter Island. For half a century between the 1890s to the 1940s, my family leased Rapa Nui (as its denizens called it) from the Chilean government and ran it as a company island.

We turned one of the most remote peopled places on Earth into a sheep and cattle station on the Australian model. The remaining Rapa Nui at the time of our arrival numbered around a hundred souls, their ranks decimated from historical norms by civil violence, disease and Peruvian blackbirders, while their language, mores and historical imagination had been sundered and warped by Catholic missionaries and colonial diktat.

These people, who had already suffered so much, were restricted to the encampment of Hanga Roa, with the remainder of the island set aside for grazing. The main English manager of that time took two Rapa Nui wives while in charge of Rapa Nui, the second when she was in her mid-teens. Meanwhile, shepherds from Scotland brought in to care for mobs of Merinos imported from New South Wales tore down ancient ceremonial platforms and used the stones for dry walls like those at home.

The Rapa Nui could get work during shearing season, or perhaps help mustering cattle. But their meagre pay could only be spent on expensive items at the company store. Their Vincent Lingiari was a woman with the daunting sobriquet María Angata Veri Tahi ‘a Pengo Hare Koho. In 1914, around the outbreak of war, Angata began receiving messages from God (she'd been a catechist on Papeete for a time, before returning to her home island) that told her Rapa Nui had been returned to its people. She led the islanders on a series of raids against livestock belonging to the firm. Great feasts followed, collective resistance manifesting as a form of potlatch, with animal carcasses left scattered across the island. The company had to call the Chilean Navy in to restore order.

The uprising Angata led was not the end of company rule – far from it. But her rebellion obliged Chile to take greater responsibility for the islanders over time. It was the beginning of what we could call the land rights movement for the Rapa Nui, a movement that continues to this day.

~

I knew bare rumours of Easter Island as a child. It was only when a great aunt in England made a gift to me of a fish carved from mahoe wood by a Rapa Nui artist in the 1930s that the story began to reveal itself. I have since spent years researching this period, visiting Chile (the port city of Valparaíso was Balfour Williamson's home base) and Rapa Nui, trying to understand the true scope and nature of what unfolded there, and shape a book around it.

Whatever caveats I've managed to carve out for my family in relation to this tiny footnote to their international concerns, I can only admit their guilt – and mine by descent. What happened on Rapa Nui was what happened to Indigenous Australians. Here was a distilled version of the same displacement, forced assimilation, economic immiseration and so on. It could have as easily been the Gulf Country as the Eastern Pacific.

Just as Kate Grenville is obliged in *Unsettled* to reckon with the fact that her family were likely direct agents of frontier violence – and just as David Marr was forced to make public in 2023's *Killing for Country* his own forebears' murderous acts against Indigenous peoples in Queensland – I came to appreciate that there was to be no ducking of the truth for my family either. As the grizzled *Guardian* correspondent I interviewed about Rapa Nui in Santiago a decade ago said to me: 'Know this: your family weren't the good guys.'

I tell this story late in the text both because I feel disquiet at the awkward 'positioning' that writers who have privilege sometimes undertake – it risks looking like self-aggrandisement, just couched in the negative – and because I wanted Alexis's work to be front and centre throughout. But I cannot finish without explaining, in apologetic retrospection, why her work is so personally important and necessary to me.

~

Wright's fiction posits what she calls a great 'brokenness' in the world. That brokenness is expressed in ecological terms – that dust pall over Praiseworthy is only the latest instance – but these are physical, visible symptoms of what is closer to a spiritual malaise. The settler-colonial enterprise in Australia has done such harm because it is founded upon first principles – greed and exploitation, without thought for sustaining human presence here – that are evidence of some intrinsic moral sickness, a pride grown monstrously outsized.

You might think the implicit message of Wright's fiction would, then, be debilitating for any thoughtful non-Indigenous audience: a form of readerly masochism. But while her fiction can be stern, even furious in denunciation, as I've suggested, her books can be warm, sly, joyful and simply exquisite too. The very fact of their existence – written in English, directed at an educated audience of global readers – means that they are, at heart, an invitation to listen and a request to be heard.

In *Carpentaria*, thinking of the way in which the character Norm Phantom keeps a library of stories in his head to be ready to trade with others, Wright calls this willingness to share *decorum*: 'the good information, intelligence, etiquette of the what to do, how to behave … how to live like a proper human being, alongside spirits for neighbours in dreams.'

There is, of course, no separating this particular teller of tales from the patch of Country from which those stories come. But like any great regional writer – from Ireland's John McGahern to Mississippi's William Faulkner – it's from the distinctly local that Wright gleans universals. Wright's fiction is an opportunity to observe an Indigenous author of talent and command thinking at global scale about those issues affecting not just the author's community but us all.

~

For we are all embodied. We come from the Earth and return to it; we all take part in the enigma of existence. The difference between black and white worlds in this story is a recent aggrandisement on the part of Europeans. Once they, too, saw themselves in proper relation to the world. They understood themselves to be a minor part of the grand canvas of creation and comported themselves with due humility. They lived within limits and encoded the virtue of doing so in morality and religion.

With the emergence of the carbon economy and the rise of industrialisation in the West, those limits were first weakened, then demolished. There was no corner of the Earth we could not access, annex and exploit – no aspect of the natural world we could not tame, dam, redirect, reshape or mine according to our needs. We no longer saw ourselves as part of the world. Rather we were above the world, its masters.

Australia is a neo-European settler society founded on a continent immensely rich in those resources a hungry and busy world desires. As such, it has not been in the interest of settlers to think hard about their place here. To consider the implications of their actions for Australia's First Peoples, or for the environment, would be too expensive and time-consuming; too potentially messy in outcome. Our present moment – in which brumby populations can rise by up to twenty-five per cent a year while ancient Gondwanaland forests burn in climate-accelerated fires and the Great Barrier Reef, largest living creature on Earth, suffers its fifth bleaching event in eight years – is the downstream result of that failure of consideration.

But Alexis's fiction imagines an alternative. It depicts groups for whom citizenship is inextricably linked to stewardship of place, not a licence to exploit. So, too, do her novels embrace the contradictions that shape any society and which must be accommodated in decision-making about the future. She displays a concomitantly powerful disdain for binary thinking in politics and the media.

And as she shows so powerfully in *Tracker*, individual autonomy is a virtue, but such autonomy must, of necessity, be enacted through a social order; the individual only comes into distinctiveness in relation to others. Europeans used to agree that no man was an island.

Most significantly, Wright's fiction (and here I think of the government of Warren Finch in *The Swan Book*) expresses deep suspicion of thrones, hierarchies – the entire perpendicular architecture of Western power. I find it hard to imagine that, over the course of Indigenous Australia's immense history, people never explored other social configurations or ways of arranging power. I like to think that they tried vertical hierarchies and found them unfit for purpose, even distasteful.

There is always a sense (think of Norm Phantom, think of Widespread) that leaders in

Wright's novels are subject to a degree of scorn and *lèse-majesté* that seems unfair, even overdone. I propose that this is because tall poppy syndrome is not an aspect of white Australia's love of egalitarianism and the fair go but a powerful necessity for survival among First Australians before European arrival.

~

Such is the well I drink from when I read Alexis Wright. Yes, I feel condemned when I absorb her books; it's hard not to feel arraigned when so much hurt lingers into our present political and social compact. But what is crucial here is that guilt is a starting point and not an end designed for some self-loathing middle-class audience to marinate in – that would be the true and final decadence.

For those of us who feel a direct relation to historical wrongdoing, Wright offers a blueprint for alternative ways of living and thinking: ones that are both immensely practical and metaphysically expansive. She gives us a way to rethink our relationship to Country and she suggests means by which we might order the world so that it is fairer, kinder, more disciplined and amenable to collective survival.

Even for those readers who, by happy accident, evade connection to the damage effected upon Indigenous Australians by European presence, Wright has news. Modernity is a cage that traps us all. The recycling bin's contents destined for landfill outside Jakarta. The plastics none of us are allowed to quit.

Wright is not fussy in the community she seeks to grow. Do you have a heart? her books ask. Is it still beating? *Do you want to live*? If the answer is yes, she says, then you're with me. There is something exhilarating in the breadth of her church. For a congenital doomscroller with ancestor issues like myself, Alexis opens a door to the potential for justice, comity and healing. It's one I walk through with gratitude and relief.

ACKNOWLEDGEMENTS

I'd like to first thank the editors of the Review section of *The Weekend Australian* – including Stephen Romei, Caroline Overington and Tim Douglas – who over many years indulged and encouraged my interest in Indigenous literature in general and Alexis's writing in particular. Portions of this book are drawn from essays and reviews first published in *The Weekend Australian*, including 'The Voice and the Canon' (2022) and individual notices of *The Swan Book* (2013), *Tracker* (2018) and *Praiseworthy* (2024). Parts of this work were also first published in the twenty-fifth-anniversary edition of *Plains of Promise*, published by UQP in 2022.

This book was long in the reading and writing; as such, it has many parents. I'm lucky to have writer friends and colleagues whose duty of care to the natural world is sincere and thoughtful. In this pantheon of decency I include James

Bradley, Delia Falconer, Matt Lamb, Jane Rawson, Johanna Bell, Richard Flanagan and Gregory Day, though there are many others. Beyond all, I owe dues to Robert Macfarlane, friend to both Alexis and myself – Rob, you point the way.

The Indigenous writers I praise in these pages are not only names, but authors I review or publish, or claim friendship with. Warm gratitude to Tony Birch for throwing me under the bus to write this book – and firm affection to Picador author Kim Scott, whose account of an evening of magpie goose over an open fire and yarns with Tracker and Alexis has stayed with me ever after. Tara June, bless you for the negroni afternoons. Alexis, your generosity in allowing me to write about you and your work over the years is an honour and a responsibility I don't deserve. My gratitude to you is eternal.

Two scholars, in particular, have shaped this corner of my reading ecosystem: Emeritus Professor William Christie of ANU taught me how to think about European Romanticism in relation to antipodean space, while Ivor Indyk showed me how to be an entrepreneur of serious culture. He also, as lecturer, once obliged me to read Samuel Richardson's 1500-page novel *Clarissa*, presumably in preparation for the mighty trek through Alexis's fiction. Ivor, I know Alexis will welcome the fact that this book is dedicated to you.

A publisher myself, I know a tricky author when I meet them. Chris Feik, most gently cerebral of Australian publishers, allow me to apologise in public for my dilatory ways. Kate Hatch, editor extraordinaire, thank you for making the edits a frictionless delight. The work of Black Inc. only grows more important over time. And to my colleagues at Pan Macmillan Australia, thank you for indulging my side hustles; you're the finest co-workers anyone could ask for.

This book was written on unceded Gadigal, Wiradjuri and Palawa lands.

BOOKS BY ALEXIS WRIGHT

FICTION

Plains of Promise (1997)

Carpentaria (2006)

The Swan Book (2013)

Praiseworthy (2023)

NON-FICTION

Grog War (1997)

Take Power, Like This Old Man Here: An Anthology of Writings Celebrating Twenty Years of Land Rights in Central Australia, 1977–1997 (editor, 1998)

Tracker (2017)